THE ULTIMATE FAN BOOK
OLIVIA RODRIGO

EVERYTHING YOU NEED TO KNOW ABOUT THE WORLD'S HOTTEST POP STAR

INDEPENDENT & UNOFFICIAL

WELBECK

CONTENTS

INTRODUCTION

In January 2021, while the COVID-19 pandemic continued to spread across the globe, Olivia Rodrigo became the world's most popular teenager and the planet's most famous popstar.

For many of her newfound fans it was an overnight success. For Olivia, it was the wish fulfilment of a decade-long dream that began with writing songs in her bedroom at the age of five.

In just one month, Olivia's deliciously autobiographical and authentic debut pop-rock track 'drivers license' launched Olivia not only to the top of the U.S. charts (with the rest of the world charts quick to follow) but also into the homes of billions – *yes, billions!* – of streamers whose hearts had been smashed into smithereens, just like Olivia's. They had found a new soundtrack to their heartache.

Skip forward to the start of 2022, a year after the release of her breakout single, and six months after her critically acclaimed and record-breaking debut album *Sour*, Olivia's universe – and the social media spaces occupied by her and her new fans, or Livvies, as they love to be labelled – had changed beyond all recognition.

Olivia Rodrigo, *the songwriter*, was now everyone's favourite new star.

'drivers license' became the biggest streamed/viewed and downloaded song of the year, breaking all sorts of world records in the process, and *Sour* impressed pretty much everyone with its songwriting power and prowess, quickly ensuring Olivia became *Time* magazine's Entertainer of the Year. This prestigious accolade was an absolutely astonishing accomplishment for a Filipina-American teenager, the first (hopefully the first of many) to receive such a recognition.

These achievements were just the start of what would turn out to be a truly life-changing twelve months for Olivia Rodrigo. Come the close of the year, Olivia stood proud as the most-nominated artist at the American Music Awards, as well as being the frontrunner for seven(!) nominations at the Grammy Awards. Wow.

Of course, as we all know now, before Olivia blossomed into a musical behemoth, the quiet and kind teenager was an aspiring actress who "grew up on set", before becoming the breakout star on TV shows such as *High School Musical: The Musical: The Series* and *Bizaardvark*.

But when boredom and isolation struck during the COVID-19 lockdowns of 2020, Olivia, alone in her childhood bedroom, reached for the stars to find herself. All she had to do was sit at her piano and pour her heart out. She did and the songs that fell out soon became too big to be contained in her bedroom. Destiny was waiting.

From bedroom musician to aspiring actor to Disney TV star to legitimate singer-songwriter (don't call her a pop princess!), Olivia's road to fame has been as surprising as it has been inevitable. She is a pop paradox; hers is a story as unbelievable as it is true.

From representing millions of Filipino-Americans, to representing a new breed of self-made superstar, as well as being a down-to-earth artist who demands complete control in every aspect of her life, Olivia is so much more than your average child star Disney+ pop princess. As she said, "If I am ushering in a new generation of pop stars that aren't afraid to speak their mind, that's cool... I'm just doing my thing, though."

As has become very quickly apparent in such a short few years, Olivia Rodrigo is waking up every day and working hard to make her fairy-tale come true. And she's only just started.

Welcome to the super sweet (and *Sour*) world of Olivia Rodrigo...

> "I'M SO HAPPY FOR THE FIRST TIME IN SO LONG, I JUST DON'T WANT TO F*** WITH IT, YOU KNOW WHAT I MEAN? I JUST LOVE MY GIRLFRIENDS AND LOVE MY JOB AND AM EXACTLY WHERE I'VE ALWAYS WANTED TO BE. EVERYTHING ELSE IS JUST ICING ON THE CAKE."

"I'M A TEENAGE GIRL. I WRITE ABOUT STUFF THAT I FEEL REALLY INTENSELY AND I THINK THAT'S AUTHENTIC AND NATURAL. DO YOU WANT ME TO WRITE A SONG ABOUT INCOME TAXES?"

ABOVE: Olivia, aged 13, attends Amazon's celebration of *Gortimer Gibbon's Life on Normal Street*, California, 8 July 2016.

RIGHT: Olivia performs 'good 4 u' and 'drivers license' at the 2021 American Music Awards, 21 November 2021, California.

CALIFORNIA DREAMING

Olivia Rodrigo's world record-breaking, sweet-and-sour songwriting, all-singing-and-dancing career began, as so often these stories do, in the teenage bedroom of her childhood California home dreaming of a fairy-tale. It was there Olivia had "the best childhood ever", an upbringing that planted the foundations of her fairy-tale until it was ready to come true. The rest is, well...

Born on 20 February 2003, and raised in Temecula, California – "the suburbs of the suburbs," as Olivia once described it – it didn't take Olivia's parents, Sophia and Roland, long to see that their only child was a star waiting to be wished upon. Before Olivia could even string sentences together, the infant's desire to compose songs and sing to an audience – even if it was just to her pet snake, Stripes – was strong. ("They kept a f***ing snake in my bedroom when I was three years old!" Olivia said of her first friend.) Of course, Olivia didn't want to be a singer-songwriter straightaway. When playing with her American Girl dolls, and contorting them into positions, Olivia's first career dream was to be an Olympic gymnast. "I was terrible at it — terrible!" she says of her first dream now.

At home, Olivia would sing all day long, belting out the choruses to No Doubt's 'Bathwater' and the White Stripes' 'Seven Nation Army' – alternative rock songs she'd been drowned in by her music-obsessed parents. Olivia's first gig was to see the punk band Weezer, and the Cure, the Smashing Pumpkins, and her mom's favorite riot grrrl bands, all sound-tracked Olivia's youth much more than any pop pixie.

But it was three very special female singer-songwriters that inspired and influenced young Olivia the most: Lorde, Taylor Swift and Alanis Morissette. Without these iconic artists, Olivia would not exist as she does today.

"Lorde's *Pure Heroine*. When it came out, I was like 11 or 12 or something like that,' Olivia recalled in 2021. "I had the vinyl record of it. I got it from Urban Outfitters. I remember listening to the lyrics and thinking, Oh, my God – I can actually see myself in these lyrics. Listening to that record for the first time is the moment when I first remember wanting to be a songwriter. She talks about driving to the suburbs and going to school and all her friend-group drama. I remember feeling so seen: she's taking this normal experience that we all go through and turning it into something really beautiful and artful. I always wanted to write a record like that, but never felt like I had that normal life experience."

Along with Lorde, Olivia and her mother would belt out the tracks

TOP: Olivia's rock star idol, Alanis Morissette.

RIGHT: You know her name! Olivia's biggest inspiration, and new gal pal, Taylor Swift.

ABOVE: Lorde, one of Olivia's biggest musical influences: "I wanna make art like Lorde."

BELOW, LEFT: Where it all began: Olivia's hometown in all its glory –Temecula, California. Today, Olivia lives in Los Angeles.

BELOW, RIGHT: Olivia, as Nini, serenades Joshua Bassett at the piano in season one of *High School: The Musical: The Series*, 2019.

"I'M VERY PROUD OF WHO I AM AND WHERE I CAME FROM NOW. BUT GROWING UP, ME AND MY OTHER MORE ETHNIC FRIENDS GREW UP IN THIS WORLD WHERE WE THOUGHT THAT BEING A WHITE GIRL WOULD BE BETTER, AND YOU'D BE HAPPIER, AND PEOPLE WOULD LIKE YOU MORE. HOPEFULLY YOUNG GIRLS WHO FELT THE WAY THAT I DID GROWING UP CAN RELATE OR FIND CONFIDENCE AND SOLACE IN THE MUSIC THAT I WRITE. THAT WOULD BE THE COOLEST THING."

from Alanis Morissette's masterpiece, *Jagged Little Pill* (1997). The album sold more than 25 million copies, and made a huge impression on Olivia's mindscape. Today, Morissette lavishes praise on her apprentice.

"Olivia has a steadfast care about self-expression," Morissette said. "She's not precious about it, nor does she seem overwhelmed by it all." Olivia's career, thus far, shares more than a few parallels with Morissette's. Like Olivia, Morissette started out on children's TV before releasing a debut album that turned into a monster that not only defined its artist, but the world it mirrored. Two decades after its release, and with Olivia's mom playing it on repeat, its influence still remained strong. As musical idols and influences go, however, there is no better than Morissette's *JLP*, especially on the ears of young female musicians.

"I remember having my mind blown when I was 13," Olivia says of her idol's debut album. "I was in the car with my parents listening to *Jagged Little Pill*. I remember hearing 'Perfect' and I just looked at music and songwriting in a completely different way."

But, of course, it is Taylor Swift who dominates Olivia's song writing sonics the most. Much has been written about Swift's influence on Olivia's song writing – with Swift being co-credited on Olivia's 'Dejá Vu' after comparison to Taylor's 'Cruel Summer' rang too close to home. Naturally, Swift's influence can be heard on *Sour*, Olivia's debut album, in almost every song, but, as Olivia has pointed out many times, all music is created by standing on the shoulders of giants.

"I've looked up to Taylor since I was five years old. Obviously I think Taylor's the best songwriter of all time," Olivia recalled. "I think her writing every single one of her songs was a big inspiration for me. I take songwriting the most seriously out of any career that I have. It's just so important to me. And I think that's sort of the same with her. I'm like, the biggest fangirl."

Raised on a healthy diet of her parents' music, strong female songwriters, and having her own creative talent, experiences and

RIGHT: The star, aged 12, attends the "Express Yourself" benefit, 15 November 2015, California.

ABOVE: Olivia appears on the 'Young Adult' episode of *New Girl*, with Jake Johnson and Saylor Curda, 28 February 2015.

BELOW: The East High gang's all there! Left to right: Kourtney, E.J, Big Red, Nini, Ashlyn, Ricky, Carlos and Gina.

dreams to be encouraged, it wasn't long before Olivia turned her inspiration towards the piano and started composing her own songs in the hope of fame one day.

Just one problem: many of her idols didn't look like Olivia. Yes, Rihanna and Beyoncé had dominated the scene for several years, but where were all the mixed-race stars of the future? "It's hard for anyone to grow up in this media where it feels like if you don't have European features and blond hair and blue eyes, you're not traditionally pretty," said Olivia. "I felt that a lot – since I don't look exactly like the girl next door, I'm not attractive. That actually took me a while to shake off. It's something I'm still shaking off now."

The way Olivia "shook off" her feelings about the way she looked – and how under-represented Filipino-Americans are in music and TV – was, as ever, to sit down and write a song... and become the voice of those without one. According to her mom, it took Olivia a while to find write something tuneful.

"Olivia loved making up 'gibberish' songs almost from the time she could speak," her mom Sophia, a school teacher, said of her daughter's earliest songwriting days. "Once she learned how to play instruments, that's when her passion for music really escalated."

"I've been writing songs since I was five years old," Olivia remembered. "Just gibberish, stuff about getting lost in the grocery store. My mom has a lot of them on VHS tapes! I was not going to be a classical pianist. It was not my jam to learn songs that other people wrote and then play them. But I'm glad my parents forced me, because playing piano is a skill I utilize every day."

At age eight, Olivia wrote the first lyrics she remembers being proud of. "I'm a human being," and "I can clean up my own messes." Powerful stuff!

Even back then, as they do most vitally now, for Olivia's craft, words arrive before music. They inform the heartbeat, the rhythm, the mood, and the purpose. Lyrics have remained the most

RIGHT: Olivia at the Disney Channel's "The Swap", California, 5 October 2016.

OPPOSITE: Olivia joins The Simpsons clan to celebrate the launch of Disney+, California, 12 November 2019. Olivia's *driving home to you* film was launched on the streaming service on 25 March 2022.

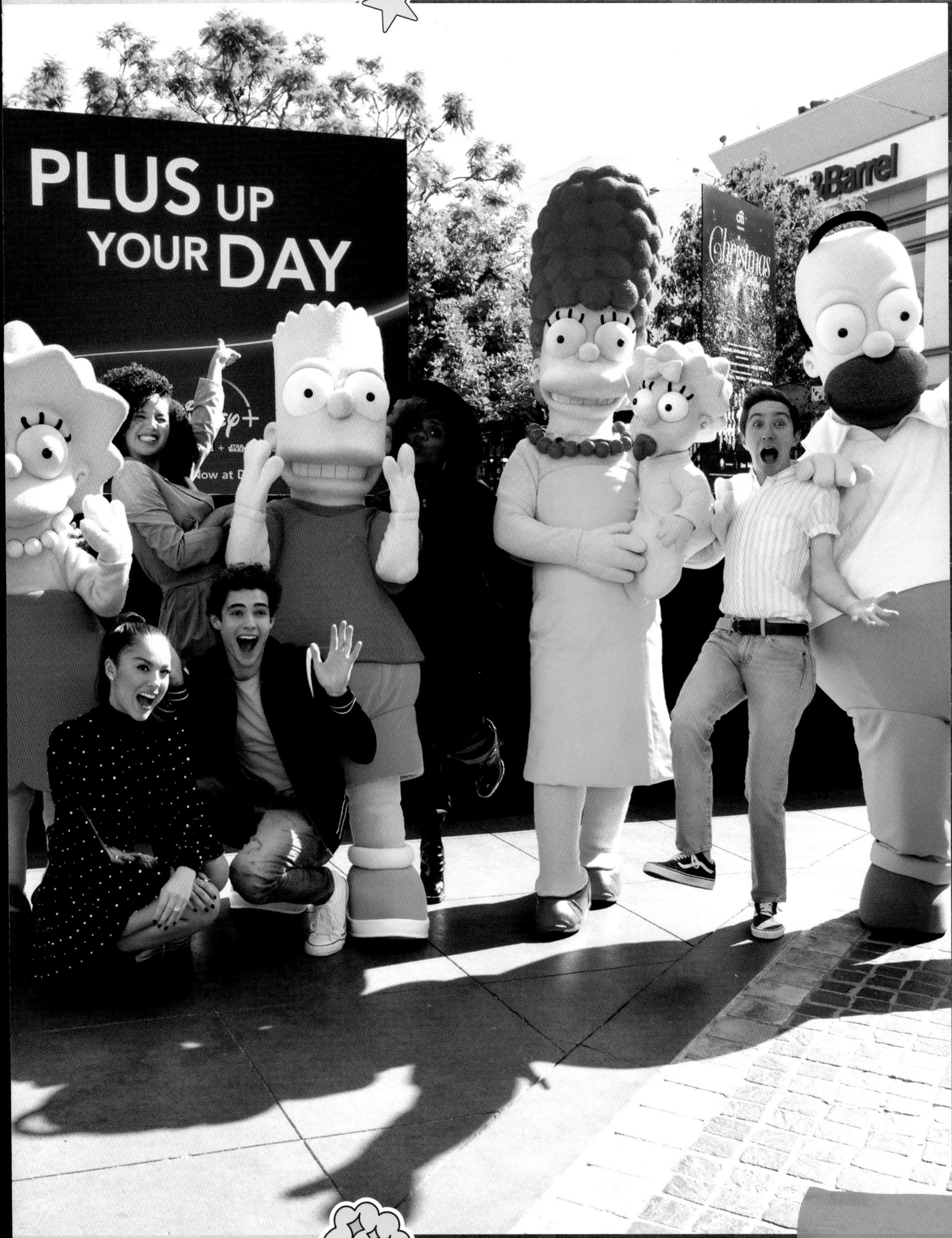
PLUS UP
YOUR DAY
Christmas

"I STILL PINCH MYSELF ABOUT MY SUCCESS EVERY DAY."

important element to Olivia's songwriting. Without truth to her words, the songs have no power. A fact evident even in her earliest compositions.

"I think the first proper song I ever wrote – the first one I finessed and that was a complete song – I was probably about 12 or 13. It was called 'Naïve Girl' and I put it on my Instagram. It's probably still out there somewhere, in the depths of the internet." The lyrics speak of the richness of intimate stories to come. "My education is built upon some 20th century daydream, I'm beginning to learn, despite the façade, that people are not always as pretty as they seem," followed by the chorus of "Little naïve girl isn't so naïve anymore." Pretty epic stuff for a 12-year-old!

With a young Olivia able to turn her emotions into music – simply by sitting down at a piano and singing how she felt – she was able to be alone in her bedroom for many years and create magic at her fingertips; a skill that would require to be utilized during the COVID lockdowns of 2020, once again giving Olivia the time and opportunity in isolation to pour her heart out at her piano. A skill that is, in her mind "therapeutic, and better than psychotherapy, especially when the modern world seems so difficult to understand or make sense of. "Whenever I'm feeling upset, I go to the piano. I go to the piano before I call a friend. You can literally create a whole song in your bedroom, and it can affect millions of people."

OPPOSITE: Olivia dazzles at the premiere of *Everything, Everything*, 6 May 2017 in Hollywood, California.

ABOVE: Olivia and BFF, Madison Hu, take aim... and fire!

RIGHT: Joshua and Olivia discuss their on-screen chemistry.

In tandem with songwriting in her bedroom, another side of Olivia's creativity began to blossom at the same time: her love of performance. Once Olivia started kindergarten she was enrolled in singing lessons and, by the age of eight, Olivia was a local talent-show regular. Olivia's ability to own a song – from ballad to heavy rock – was evident even then. "I was so dramatic," she recalls of her younger self. "There's videos on YouTube of me singing, and I'm so into it. I act everything out and I'm so performative. People always told my mom, 'You should put her in acting lessons.'"

So, her mom did.

Before long, the Rodrigo family began making 90-mile journeys to L.A. for acting auditions. And it was not Olivia's parents who pushed their child to attend every audition she could. It was Olivia. She had her mind set on her fairy-tale.

What came next, not even Olivia could have dreamed...

BREAKING FREE

Before the album, accolades, acclaim, and worldwide fame, Olivia was an aspiring 11-year-old actress waiting in line at auditions. Her fingers were forever crossed that her Filipino-American heritage, wholesome looks and raw, but rare, singing and acting talent would be just enough to win one life-changing role. The only question was: *how long would she have to wait?*

When Olivia was in seventh grade, her parents moved from Temecula to L.A. as Olivia began to more seriously, and persistently, pursue acting. From this point on, Olivia was in control of her career, lovingly supported and encouraged by her parents. Olivia pushed for any television and film acting auditions for any role she could – a "brutal" process for anyone, let alone an eleven-year-old.

"Auditions are really rough," recalled Olivia. "I know people who've gone into their first audition and booked it, but that definitely was not my experience." A month before Olivia was about

to pack it all in, Christmas 2013, and give up on her dreams, she booked her first acting gig. It couldn't have come soon enough.

At age 11, in 2014, Olivia filmed her first project, *An American Girl: Grace Stirs Up Success.* The straight-to-video movie gave Olivia the required screen-time she needed to impress executives at Disney, and bag a series lead on the Disney Channel series, *Bizaardvark.*

While the show was not something Olivia particularly enjoyed at the time, the series was a stepping stone to where she knew she wanted to be. The show revolves around two oddball 13-year-

old best friends – clumsy and kind Paige (played by Olivia) and Frankie (Madison Hu), who together write funny songs and create content for their blossoming vlog, called *Bizaardvark*. The show was a hit for Disney and ran for three years. Olivia's portrayal of guitarist Paige Olvera turned heads too, as well as introducing her to Madison, Olivia's IRL BFF. During her tenure on the show, Olivia also co-starred with the now-infamous "shock" YouTuber, Jake Paul. It was Paul who gave Olivia the confidence kick up the butt. "The last thing he said to me was, 'You're gonna sell out stadiums one day, kid.'"

Executives at Disney also spoke of the same superstar qualities that Paul did: Olivia was a true four-dimensional threat, she could sing, dance and act *and* had a genuine, natural charm which engaged with pre-teen viewers. In short: on screen, Olivia radiated superstar talent.

As a part of the Disney family, Olivia was soon cast as a series lead as Nini in *High School Musical: The Musical: The Series*, the ultra-meta reboot of the hit movies starring Zac Efron. Olivia

revealed that she would return for season three of the show, which began filming in January 2022, but won't come back after that – destiny is calling, after all.

From episode one, however, and for two seasons straight up until late 2019, Olivia was the series' MVP. Each week, she proved that she could sing all genres of songs and had an immediately engaging and charismatic presence on camera, something her *Sour* producer, Daniel Nigro, saw immediately in her too.

"You put me on camera and all of a sudden I get in my head and

OPPOSITE: Olivia shows off her incredible ukulele skills on *High School Musical: The Musical: The Series*. Remember the song?

BELOW: Olivia and Joshua run through their lines on *HSMTMTS*.

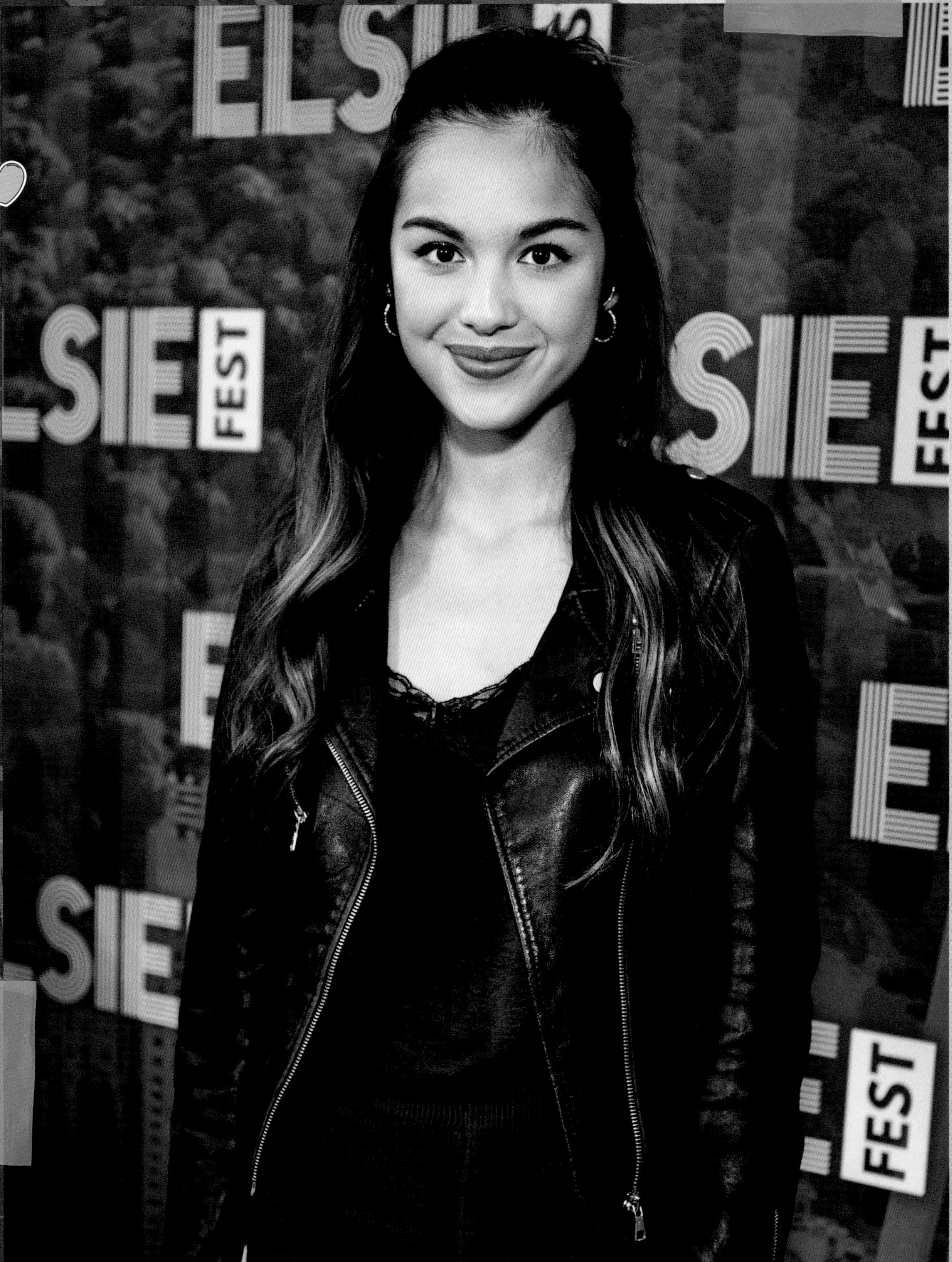
FEST
FEST

I can't perform. But with Olivia, it's the exact opposite. You'd say, 'OK, we're filming you, people are watching', and all of a sudden she gives the performance of a lifetime."

High School The Musical: The Musical: The Series gave Olivia a serious platform from which to express her voice, as well as hone her craft. "When I was shooting season two of High School Musical, I wrote five of the songs on my album." And, with her plaintive ballad 'All I Want', Olivia's singer-songwriter credentials rocketed into the stratosphere when it went viral on TikTok in late 2019 – life imitating art from her Bizaardvark days – and became the the defining hit of the show's second season. It immediately led to a deal with Interscope Records."I remember going to see a bunch of record labels and they were all wonderful. But Interscope was the only place where they said, 'We really love your songwriting abilities, we think you're a really great, classic songwriter.' And that was special to me and the start of a great relationship."

Following in the footsteps of her inspirations and idols – Britney Spears and Christina Aguilera to Selena Gomez and Demi Lovato – and with 'All I Want' out in the wild, Olivia sent out the clarion call to inform her fans of the start of the next chapter of her career. "I always thought of myself as a singer-songwriter who fell into acting and really liked it, rather than a child actor who's like, 'Oh, I'm going to try to be a pop star now,'" Olivia explained of her sudden career change.

At this juncture, Olivia became acutely aware of the labels associated with Disney child stars, and Olivia was keen, from the start, to not be pigeonholed by peers, fans and critics as the "Disney pop girl archetype".

"Some of my favourite artists came from Disney Channel, but I always wanted to do something different. I never wanted to be a pop girl; that was never my

> "IT'S SCARY TO GO FROM AN ENVIRONMENT LIKE DISNEY – WHERE EVERY DAY YOU ARE TOLD WHAT TO DO, WHAT TO SAY, WHAT TO WEAR – TO BEING AN ARTIST, WHERE YOU HAVE AN ABSOLUTE BLANK CANVAS."

OPPOSITE: Ms Rodrigo shines at Elsie Fest: Broadway's Outdoor Music Festival, New York, 5 October 2019.

RIGHT: Olivia, as Nini, and Joshua, as Richard, enjoy a kiss.

"I JUST REMEMBER BEING 14 YEARS OLD AND BEING LIKE, 'I LITERALLY HAVE NO IDEA WHO I AM. I DON'T KNOW WHAT MY PERSONAL STYLE IS. I DON'T KNOW WHAT I LIKE. I DON'T KNOW WHO MY TRUE FRIENDS ARE. HOW AM I EXPECTED TO CULTIVATE AN IMAGE?' THAT WAS ALWAYS HARD FOR ME. EVEN NOW, I HAVE NO IDEA. I TRY, BUT MY IMAGE TODAY IS NOT GOING TO BE THE IMAGE THAT I'LL PROBABLY LIKE TOMORROW."

RIGHT: Lady in red: Olivia steals the show in the now-iconic Amanda Uprichard Nia Mini Dress (in lipstick red) in "The Auditions" episode of *High School Musical: The Musical: The Series*.

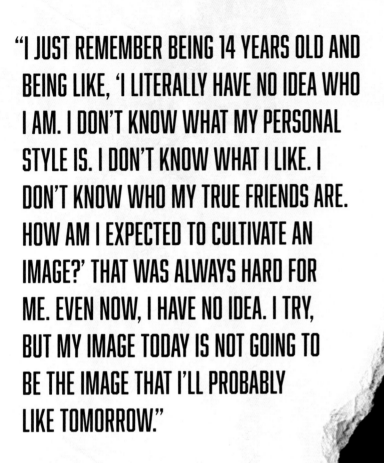

ABOVE: Olivia at the 2016 Radio Disney Music Awards, California, 30 April 2016.

OPPOSITE: Olivia and Joshua at Elsie Fest: Broadway's Outdoor Music Festival, New York, 5 October 2019.

prerogative. I always wanted to write my own songs, and it was super-important to me that I told my own stories in my unique voice. I've only ever seen myself as a songwriter. I remember the first time an article said, 'Olivia Rodrigo is the next big pop star' — I was like, there are so many things that go along with 'pop star' that I never thought I'd be. But I'll take it."

Olivia's course correction in her career also came at a strange time for the world. And perhaps without the *HSTMTMTS* lockdown production hiatus (due to the pandemic in 2020) Olivia may never have returned seriously to her musical roots. And back to her childhood bedroom, where the iconic 'drivers license' single and all the songs for her album *Sour* were created.

In December 2020, Olivia revealed to the world that she had recorded her debut single during the first wave of isolation. Her inspiration was *HSTMTMTS* co-star, and then-boyfriend, Joshua Bassett. "Joshua challenged me to write a song every day of quarantine. So, I challenged myself to be as creative as possible during lockdown." Joshua's challenge bore fruit... and awoke a songwriting monster within Olivia.

It also forged a musical collaboration that would become the most important relationship in Olivia's life for the next twelve months – not Bassett, but Daniel Nigro, her producer.

Dan Nigro and Olivia bonded immediately over a shared love of rock music. "She knows the whole Rage Against the Machine catalogue the same way I do," Nigro recalled. Nigro also respected Olivia's songwriting process even when the worldwide success

> "I THINK THERE'S A SPECIFIC ARCHETYPE OF THE DISNEY STAR TURNED POP STAR THAT I DIDN'T WANT TO FOLLOW."

of 'drivers license' meant that Olivia could have chosen to do anything she wanted. "The success made her feel empowered to do other things, which felt so mature," Nigro said. Nigro, who's previously collaborated with the likes of Lewis Capaldi, Carly Rae Jespen and Sky Ferreira, became Olivia's go-to collaborator for 'drivers license' and then *Sour*. Their collaboration began after he contacted Olivia via Insta DMs after watching a video of her singing 'happier' on Instagram. "I remember getting the chills when she sang the line 'I hope you're happy, but don't be happier,'" Nigro recalls of the moment he knew Olivia was the real deal. "There was this beautiful intensity in her voice that I fell in love with immediately. It blew me away," he said. The pair have worked together ever since – mostly in his garage. Olivia immediately took her producer and musical partner seriously when he spoke of her potential as a songwriter. Her one request? Don't watch *High School Musical*!

"I wanted Daniel to know me for me and not the side character that I was playing in a TV show. I also just get really self-conscious about stuff like that, on a human level. I hate it when my friends listen to my songs or watch anything. I get insecure about it. It's been difficult, learning to become comfortable enough with somebody to be like, 'Hi, here's all my insecurity and heartbreak, let's make a song out of it!'"

The first song to take all of Olivia's heartbreak and insecurity was, of course, 'drivers license'.

Olivia's debut single was released 8 January 8 2021 – just days before her eighteenth birthday... and, upon its release into the wild, her entire life was turned upside down.

While 'drivers license' – a song about freedom – immediately became the biggest, hottest and most popular song, the world was forced to stay at home and isolate and be less free. 'drivers license' became the song the world needed to hear at that time.

"When I came up with 'drivers license', I was going through a heartbreak that was so confusing to me, so multifaceted," Olivia recalled. "Putting all those feelings into a song made everything seem so much simpler and clearer – and at the end of the day, I think that's the whole purpose of songwriting. There's nothing like sitting at the piano in my bedroom and writing a really sad song. It's truly my favourite thing in the world."

The track, a blistering and soaring pop ballad that spins a fairy-tale romance gone dark, debuted at No.1 on the U.S. Billboard Hot 100, breaking Spotify's record, twice, for the most daily streams ever. Today, it now has more than one billion listens, more than 350 million YouTube views and shot to No.1 in 48 countries on Apple Music. Apple Music even released a statement that claimed more of its listeners read the lyrics of 'drivers license' in 2021 than read those of *any other song*, a fact that made Olivia very happy.

The song's success surprised Olivia, just as much as it did her *High School* co-stars and her high school friends. "It's quite strange because my entire life has changed in a week and also nothing has changed at all," she recalled. "Every day I'm in my house, doing my homework, but people who I've looked up to since I was 10 are reaching out and saying they love my music. It's a strange sort of paradox."

The power ballad, allegedly about her ex-boyfriend, was more than just a big chart hit. It also spoke to millions of people suffering heartbreak and loss at such a fragile time. The song changed lives. "Literally the week after 'drivers license' came out," Olivia recalled, "I was still on set for *High School Musical* and P.A.s that I never really talked to, older men, they'd come up to me and be like, 'We just went through a breakup, and this song is just changing my life – this song is exactly how I feel.' I was like, 'Oh, my God – that's so cool. You never confided in me before, but this is so cool that it has affected you.'"

The track also made Olivia's wildest dreams come true – with its immense success, Olivia transformed, almost overnight, into a legitimate singer-songwriter with street cred. "My music is definitely separate from my acting in a way I always dreamed would happen," Olivia remembered. "When 'drivers license' came

"WITH 'DRIVERS LICENSE', THERE WERE A LOT OF PEOPLE WHO WERE LIKE, 'YO, I'VE NEVER HEARD OF THIS GIRL BEFORE BUT I REALLY LIKE THIS SONG', WHICH TO ME WAS THE DREAM – TO GET A BRAND NEW INTRODUCTION TO PEOPLE JUST AS A SONGWRITER. I CONSIDER MYSELF A SONGWRITER FIRST AND I'M REALLY HAPPY THAT PEOPLE ARE STARTING TO RECOGNISE ME AS SUCH."

ABOVE: Olivia and Madison pose for a selfie with young fans at *The Descendants 2* premiere, 2017.

OPPOSITE: The big time: Olivia is A-OK at the premiere of Disney+'s *High School Musical: The Musical: The Series*, 1 November 2019.

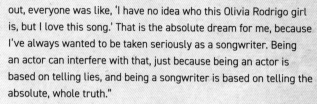

"SO MY SONG IS NO.1, AND I'M STAYING UP TILL TWO IN THE MORNING TO DO MY STATISTICS HOMEWORK!"

out, everyone was like, 'I have no idea who this Olivia Rodrigo girl is, but I love this song.' That is the absolute dream for me, because I've always wanted to be taken seriously as a songwriter. Being an actor can interfere with that, just because being an actor is based on telling lies, and being a songwriter is based on telling the absolute, whole truth."

And, of course, with the inclusion of the word "f***" in the song, Olivia was able to immediately distance herself from the Disney pop princess vision others had of her. "People always ask me, "Oh, did you say f*** in 'drivers license' to show that you aren't just a Disney star?" It's cool that people might think that, but I'm just making music that I love and that I feel passionate about. It's who I am. I have a dirty mouth. It was what felt natural and good to me, and people resonated with that."

With the world now waking up to Olivia Rodrigo the songwriter, Olivia now faced the biggest challenge of her career so far: *What on earth will she do next?*

LEFT: East High School students attend the premiere of Disney+'s *High School Musical: The Musical: The Series*, 1 November 2019.

ABOVE: Olivia performs at Elsie Fest: Broadway's Outdoor Music Festival, New York, 5 October 2019.

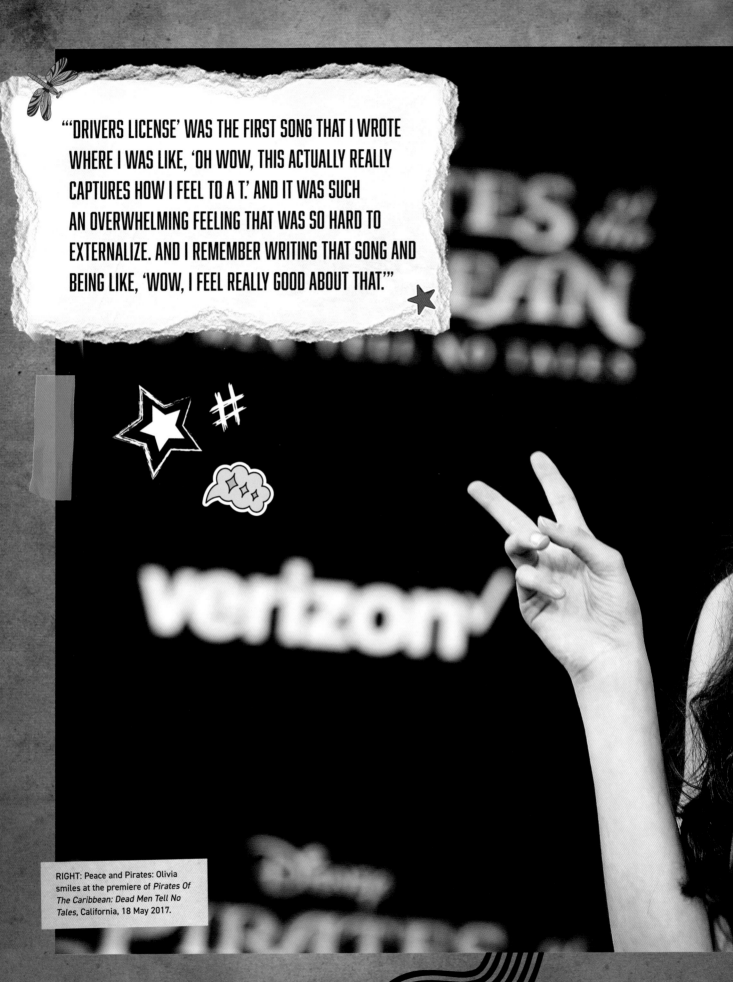

"'DRIVERS LICENSE' WAS THE FIRST SONG THAT I WROTE WHERE I WAS LIKE, 'OH WOW, THIS ACTUALLY REALLY CAPTURES HOW I FEEL TO A T.' AND IT WAS SUCH AN OVERWHELMING FEELING THAT WAS SO HARD TO EXTERNALIZE. AND I REMEMBER WRITING THAT SONG AND BEING LIKE, 'WOW, I FEEL REALLY GOOD ABOUT THAT.'"

RIGHT: Peace and Pirates: Olivia smiles at the premiere of *Pirates Of The Caribbean: Dead Men Tell No Tales*, California, 18 May 2017.

SWEET AND SOUR

Following the shock and awe of the sudden critical and commercial acclaim levelled at 'drivers license', Olivia – everyone's favourite new "spicy Pisces" – and her musical partner Daniel Nigro now had the confidence to make *Sour* as envisioned in Olivia's imagination. But, even though the world was at her command, Olivia, impressively, kept her feet planted squarely on the ground. "I don't want to be the biggest pop star that ever lived," she said. "I just want to be a songwriter."

'drivers license' opened the castle doors to Olivia's fairy-tale dream of becoming a serious and respected songwriter, but she still had to contend with the fear of being a one-hit wonder. And rather than simply knock out a whole album of songs that sounded the same as her first single, Olivia, forever the perfectionist, put the hours in with Daniel Nigro, her producer, to ensure every song had a sonic fingerprint unlike any other. Like true era-defining artists who pushed the envelope, and her idols such as Alanis Morissette and Taylor Swift, Olivia refused to be tethered to one particular sound, genre or emotion. "I hope people are surprised by *Sour*," she recalled. "I am so inspired by so many different genres of music. I love country music so much, and I love rock music so much. And obviously pop music is my favourite. But, in 2021, I feel like artists aren't really boxed into a genre anymore. I look at someone like Billie Eilish, who I'm so obsessed with, and her music is like pop, but it's kind of rock, too."

The unprecedented triumph of 'drivers license' was so epic that it gave Olivia the artistic confidence to jettison the proposed EP her label wanted and dive straight into a long-player. "I was like, 'I wish that I can make a project that fully encompasses who I am as an artist'," Olivia told her label, Interscope. "And I feel like the EP format wasn't my strongest work." Keen to fully showcase her skills as a songwriter, she was upfront and honest with Interscope, and asked if she could extend the project to a full album. Thankfully, they said yes – a decision that has paid off hugely.

Thankfully, Olivia – ever the prolific-perfectionist – had half the album written already too. And Daniel Nigro, her *Sour* soulmate was there by her side, a producer who she trusted to see her vision fully realized. "I absolutely love working with Dan. We have such a good groove together," Olivia told *Billboard* in 2022. "We are always sharing ideas back-and-forth. The craziness of *Sour* being out in the world was something that really only Dan and I could relate to, and I think that has brought us closer together. I

BELOW: "I had fallen in love with making music again," Dan Nigro said of producing Olivia's *Sour* songs.

OPPOSITE: Live on the Daytime Stage at the 2021 iHeartRadio Music Festival at AREA15, Las Vegas, 18 September 2021.

"I WRITE SOLELY FOR MYSELF. IF I TRIED TO SIT DOWN AT THE PIANO AND BE LIKE, 'I'M GOING TO WRITE A SONG THAT EVERYONE LIKES AND THAT RESONATES WITH PEOPLE!' IT'S NEVER ANY GOOD."

"NOTHING IN MUSIC IS EVER NEW. THERE'S FOUR CHORDS IN EVERY SONG. THAT'S THE FUN PART – TRYING TO MAKE THAT YOUR OWN."

trust him so much and really enjoy the music we've been making."

Nigro found something in Olivia that he was looking for too, a visionary who wasn't afraid to push away from her Disney+ past and strive for true innovation. "Olivia takes songwriting more seriously than anybody I've ever met," recalled Nigro. "Her attention to detail is just incredible. Olivia will rewrite and rewrite until she feels like every line makes total sense for what the song is trying to say. She's one of the hardest working people I've ever been with in the studio. Most singers nowadays want to lay down three or four takes and then have the attitude of 'Oh, you can fix it later, right?' But Olivia's hyper-critical," Nigro said. "She will go over every detail and inflection."

Released on 21 May 2021, *Sour* debuted at No.1 on the U.S. *Billboard* charts. General consensus among reviewers and critics alike is that *Sour* received "universal acclaim", as proved by securing Apple Music and the People's Choice's prestigious "Album of the Year" awards. The *NME* reviewed the album as millions of Olivia's fans felt was true: "An almost-masterpiece that's equal parts confident, cool and exhilaratingly real," which perfectly sums up Olivia too.

More than a year later, *Sour* still rides high in the charts and listeners' minds, accumulating awards, fans, nominations and applause – and even a documentary entitled *Driving Home 2 U (A Sour Film)* released in Spring 2022 on Disney+, a behind-the-scenes and intimate sneak-peek at the recording process of the eleven songs. A perfect flourish to finish the record's success and celebrate *Sour's* 2.5 million copies sold in the U.S., a feat that makes it the bestselling album of 2021 by a female artist. Take that, Taylor!

With all the sweet whispers said and praise heaped on *Sour*, a burning question remains why Olivia titled her first album with such an unusual downbeat title for a pop record, and the meaning

OPPOSITE, ABOVE: Dreams come true: Olivia performs an intimate 'drivers license' to a spellbound BRIT Awards audience, London, 8 February, 2021.

OPPOSITE, BELOW: Singing her heart out at the 2021 iHeartRadio Music Festival.

LEFT: Going global: Olivia becomes the youngest artist EVER to score the Official UK Chart double, for debut album *Sour* and single 'good 4 u', 28 May 2021.

behind it. Thankfully, Olivia revealed all. And the answer, as ever, gives insight into Olivia's songwriter mindset: she didn't want the title to be too, well, sweet. Because that wouldn't be the truth about the songs. "I'm obsessed with the concept of awesome things in my life – like my relationship with myself and with others – progressively going sour as I get older," Olivia revealed, hinting at the depths of her songwriting soul. "'Sour' is a very visceral word, one that captures the sounds that I'm inspired by and a specific slice of my life at 17. Plus it has my initials in it, which is a bonus!"

One of the loudest salutes for *Sour's* success is not just that it has been lauded by pop critics (who usually have their claws sharpened for former Disney child stars' first musical outings), but how the songs resonate and engage meaningfully across multiple generations. These range from pre-teen girls and boys dreaming of their teen crushes, and Gen Z discovering heartbreak for the first time, to millennial moms in love and Gen X dads who can hear the influences of their youth in Olivia's nineties rock sonics.
Sour also contains all the overwhelming emotions that a teenage girl such as Olivia, along with the largest volume of her fans, would experience in a usual week of being themselves – a rollercoaster of emotions that come with being 18 years old. Olivia

ABOVE: Posing in the media room at her first BRIT Awards, London, 11 May 2021.

RIGHT: Singing 'drivers license' at a colourful, socially distanced BRIT Awards, London, 11 May 2021.

> ## "*SOUR* IS ME GRAPPLING WITH LOVE AND HEARTBREAK AND HOW YOU FIT INTO THE WORLD AND HOW YOU RELATE TO OTHER PEOPLE. IT WASN'T SOMETHING I WROTE IN HINDSIGHT. IT'S VERY MUCH HOW I WAS FEELING AT THAT TIME. I NEEDED TO WRITE THOSE SONGS TO PROCESS THOSE EMOTIONS."

ABOVE: Olivia slows the pace at the 2021 iHeartRadio Music Festival at AREA15, Las Vegas, 18 September 2021.

OPPOSITE: Olivia is all smiles in the media room at her first BRIT Awards, London, 8 February 2021.

wanted her debut album to not only transect all the genres of music that she grew up on, because she is not a manufactured product cut from the same cloth as her peers, but also the wealth of emotions she felt bombarded with every day. "Being angry, jealous, overly emotional or sad can often be framed as being bitchy or moany," Olivia said. "I decided to shine a light on those feelings, even though that was uncomfortable to talk about."

Sour has something for everyone, an attribute that most debut records from former Disney pop princesses have rarely attempted before. For Olivia, she was laser-focused on the intention and messaging behind the songs, employing her "alternative" actorly upbringing and channelling it into the songs, rather than fighting it. The result was a wide-ranging output of emotion and genre. "I feel like music is becoming increasingly genreless," Olivia said. "I suppose I'm considered a pop artist, but I've never felt like one. I wanted *Sour* to be super versatile. My dream is to have it be an intersection between mainstream pop, folk music, and alternative pop. I love the songwriting and the lyricism and the melodies of folk music. I love the tonality of alt-pop. So I'm going to try and take all of my sort of influences … and make something that I like."

Each of the eleven incredible tracks on *Sour* arrived in Olivia's mind over a period of five months, from December 2020 to May 2021, with Olivia writing and recording during thirteen-hour days, six days a week. She wrote a song every day for the first four months of quarantine, as well while on hiatus from her *HSMTMTS* day job. The time afforded by the pandemic helped too, allowing

Olivia to studio test the songs until they were better than good enough. "I think because of the pandemic we were oddly very fortunate to have as much time as we did to make music," recalled Nigro. "I'm not sure if I could say the same if life was running at a normal pace. With less distractions we were really able to work on a song... take time off from it, go back and redo things about it if it didn't feel right and grow together as a team and find a real groove."

But it wasn't just good timing that Olivia had on her side. She also had a belief, that every one of the songs had to be true to itself, and to her vision that they should feel like proper, timeless labours of love, not just forgettable, copy-paste hits. Anything less and the song was ditched. "I write all of my lyrics from my heart and my life first."

She wrote at her family's home in L.A. (in late 2021, Olivia moved to her own home not too far away) on her brand new Yamaha piano, her first big purchase bought with her own money from *HSMTMTS*'s success. Here, Olivia felt safe inside her childhood bedroom, giving her the comfort blanket she required to truly let her demons, vulnerabilities and insecurities come out of Pandora's box. With no parameters or walls to hide behind, Olivia was free to write however, and about whatever, came into her

OPPOSITE: Olivia waves to her adoring fans at the 2021 iHeartRadio Music Festival at AREA15, Las Vegas, 18 September 2021.

TOP: Olivia stuns in a statement fluorescent Dior dress backstage at the BRIT Awards, London, 8 February 2021. ABOVE: Kicking off Instagram and

Facebook's Creator Week by showing off those legendary platform boots, 8 June 2021.

"GOING INTO THE STUDIO AND BEING LIKE, 'WHAT DO I ACTUALLY WANT THIS ALBUM TO SOUND LIKE?' AND 'WHAT DOES BIG PRODUCTION SOUND LIKE, IS THAT MY THING?' WAS A LEARNING CURVE AND A LITTLE BIT OF A CHALLENGE AT FIRST."

LEFT: Olivia waves to her adoring fans at the 2021 iHeartRadio Music Festival at AREA15, Las Vegas, 18 September 2021.

ABOVE: Another now-famous Yves Saint Laurent dress, this time at the 2021 Met Gala Celebrating In America, New York, 13 September 2021.

open mind, leading to a very personal and intimate songwriting experience, where lyrics and feelings take precedent over sparse, minimalist sonic landscapes. Upon hearing the production of 'drivers license' for the first time, Olivia realized she didn't have to go aurally bombastic to make a dent in the listeners' hearts. She could go small, minimal, sparse. "Maybe I can produce a song out and it doesn't have to feel unnecessarily poppy or big and doesn't have to feel saturated in the way that I thought it would," she said of her now-iconic sparse sound. But the lyrics, as ever, all started at home: "I literally write all of my songs right in my bedroom, looking out the window. Lyrics and melody come at the same time. I like having the first seeds of ideas come from just me. I like having a concept, or a poem, and going in with that. I don't actually think that I'm a great songwriter – I'm just a really prolific songwriter, and I write so much that some of them just have to be good. Like statistically, some of them have to work!"

The songwriting process of Olivia's favourite song on *Sour*, 'traitor', for example, shows off her distinct and authentic approach to crafting her own songs. It starts with conjuring up a memory, and then letting the emotion take control of the rest. For 'traitor', Olivia was hiking with her mom in Salt Lake City (where she was filming *HSMTMTS*) when all of a sudden the hook pops into her head: "Guess you didn't cheat, but you're still a traitor." Storing the line on her iPhone notes, Olivia completed the song

"SUCCESS IN MY EYES WOULD BE MAKING MUSIC THAT I FEEL REALLY PROUD OF, AND I FEEL LIKE IT CHALLENGES ME AND EXCITES ME AND HOPEFULLY MAKES PEOPLE FEEL UNDERSTOOD."

RIGHT: Olivia stuns in *that* YSL dress at The Academy Museum of Motion Pictures Opening Gala, California, 25 September 2021.

OPPOSITE: Olivia with country superstar Kacey Musgraves at the 2021 Met Gala Celebrating In America, New York, 13 September 2021.

ABOVE: Performing 'drivers license' in a red Dior dress at her first BRIT Awards, with harp and piano, London, 11 May 2021. OPPOSITE: Olivia drives her fans crazy during a live performance in Austin, Texas. Olivia's lovely fans are known as "Livies".

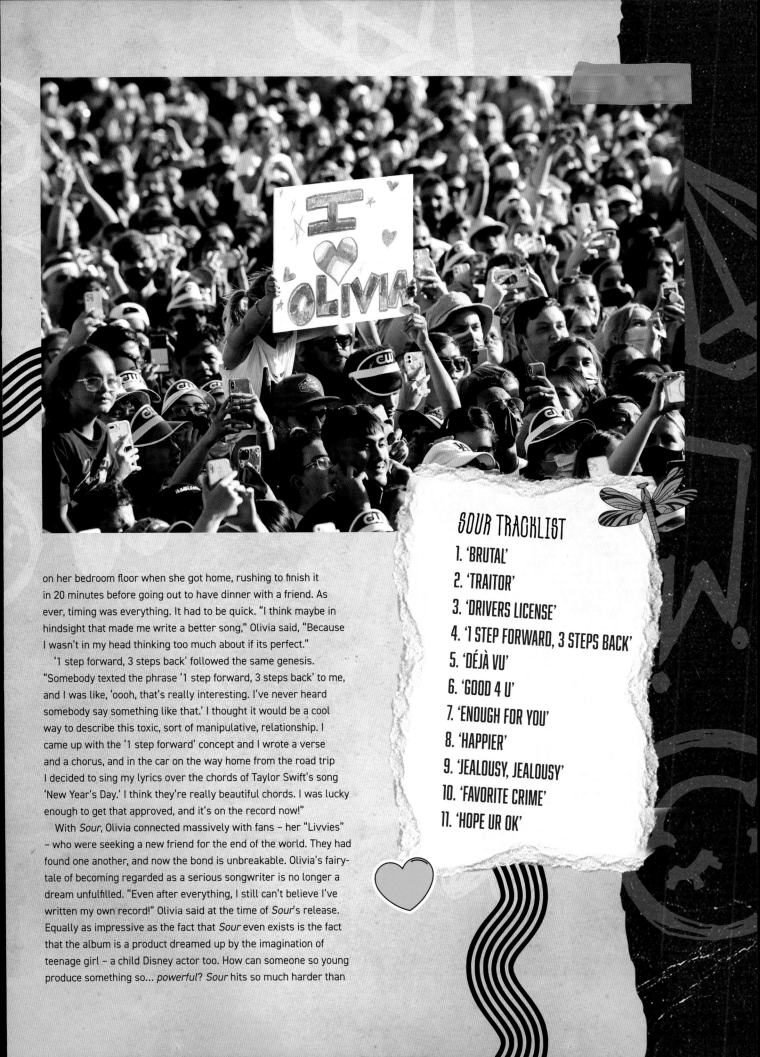

on her bedroom floor when she got home, rushing to finish it in 20 minutes before going out to have dinner with a friend. As ever, timing was everything. It had to be quick. "I think maybe in hindsight that made me write a better song," Olivia said, "Because I wasn't in my head thinking too much about if its perfect."

'1 step forward, 3 steps back' followed the same genesis. "Somebody texted the phrase '1 step forward, 3 steps back' to me, and I was like, 'oooh, that's really interesting. I've never heard somebody say something like that.' I thought it would be a cool way to describe this toxic, sort of manipulative, relationship. I came up with the '1 step forward' concept and I wrote a verse and a chorus, and in the car on the way home from the road trip I decided to sing my lyrics over the chords of Taylor Swift's song 'New Year's Day.' I think they're really beautiful chords. I was lucky enough to get that approved, and it's on the record now!"

With *Sour*, Olivia connected massively with fans – her "Livvies" – who were seeking a new friend for the end of the world. They had found one another, and now the bond is unbreakable. Olivia's fairy-tale of becoming regarded as a serious songwriter is no longer a dream unfulfilled. "Even after everything, I still can't believe I've written my own record!" Olivia said at the time of *Sour*'s release. Equally as impressive as the fact that *Sour* even exists is the fact that the album is a product dreamed up by the imagination of teenage girl – a child Disney actor too. How can someone so young produce something so... *powerful*? *Sour* hits so much harder than

SOUR TRACKLIST

1. 'BRUTAL'
2. 'TRAITOR'
3. 'DRIVERS LICENSE'
4. '1 STEP FORWARD, 3 STEPS BACK'
5. 'DÉJÀ VU'
6. 'GOOD 4 U'
7. 'ENOUGH FOR YOU'
8. 'HAPPIER'
9. 'JEALOUSY, JEALOUSY'
10. 'FAVORITE CRIME'
11. 'HOPE UR OK'

anyone was expecting, a truth not lost on its creator. "Something I'm really proud of is that this record talks about emotions that are hard to talk about or aren't really socially acceptable especially for girls: anger, jealousy, spite, sadness, they're frowned-upon as bitchy and moaning and complaining or whatever. But I think they're such valid emotions," Olivia said. "I made a project that I feel really proud of and that's the only thing that I set out to do. I try not to write songs through the lens of hoping that they're commercially successful. I just feel that takes away some of the magic of the songs."

At the start of 2022, as Olivia began ramping up her promotion for her first ever live tour, rumour began to spread of Olivia's next album. The prolific songwriter, it seems, has yet to take a day off. "I have a title for my next album and a few songs," Olivia said during rehearsals of her first tour. "And no, it's not *Sweet*!" Olivia predicts that her next album is "probably going to be a lot happier than the record I just made. My tastes are always changing, and I think that will be reflected in the next album," she said. "I'm gonna take my time to figure out exactly what I want to say and how I want to say it."

"It's definitely a different experience writing a second album after having a debut that was so well received," she continued. "It's really exciting to think about the next world that's coming up for me. I'm trying not to put too much pressure on myself...just sort of explore and have fun right now. I still write so much of my music in my bedroom though, and I don't think

that experience will ever change. Writing songs will hopefully always be an outlet for me to process my feelings before anything else."

Olivia's next album has the whole world waiting with bated breath and eager ears. But, until that monster drops, the singer-songwriter is keeping busy with all sorts of exciting adventures...

ABOVE: Olivia chats all things *Sour* and success on *Jimmy Kimmel Live!* in Los Angeles, 26 October 2021.

OPPOSITE: Olivia stuns in *that* YSL dress at The Academy Museum of Motion Pictures Opening Gala, California, 25 September 2021.

DRIVING THE WORLD CRAZY

With *Sour* leaving an indelible imprint on popular culture, and Olivia's place in the pantheon of pre-eminent popstars assured – as well as the planet's slow return to business as usual after the pandemic – Olivia has turned her attention to the future, in particular dealing with her mega-fame, touring, meeting her idols, performing and promoting the album on a plethora of TV shows. Oh, there was also that little matter of being invited to the White House to meet the President of the United States. No big deal, right?

"It was crazy. It was the most surreal experience I've had in the last year. And I've had some really surreal experiences in the last year!" Olivia recalled of her famous July 2021 invite to the White House to speak with President Joe Biden and promote the COVID-19 vaccination programme. "The White House is incredible!"

As the phenomenal popstar success story of the post-pandemic era, it seemed appropriate that Olivia be the first person the White House called to be their famous face of the nation's recovery from COVID-19. So many millions of fans relied on both *Sour* and Olivia's voice to help pull them through 2020 and 2021, that Olivia speaking from the White House press podium became headline news. Olivia now had star power, influence and more than 20 million Insta followers.

"I went to the White House for a really great cause," Olivia said of her historic moment. "It's so important that people at my age are getting vaccinated and it was really awesome that they lent me their platform. And I lent mine. I guess we kind of worked together to spread that message. It was a really meaningful moment for me. And, obviously, I got to meet the president of the United States!"

"Thank you for using your voice," the clearly impressed President said in an Insta post. He was no doubt delighted with the fact that Olivia's voice – and ability to transcend generation, race and division – helped increase national vaccination results that month.

Shortly before Olivia's Oval Office trip, the songwriter ticked off another item off of her fairy-tale bucket list – she performed her first ever live show. But, because this is Olivia's fairy-tale, her first live show was anything but ordinary – or small-scale. It was at the 2021 BRIT Awards in London – the biggest and most glamorous night in music in the whole of the UK! And instead of just a few drunk punters watching, the whole world tuned in to see their new

favourite "spicy Pisces" perform live for the very first time.

The magnitude of the night was not lost on Olivia. "It's absolutely mind-blowing! I was so nervous rehearsing for it and my team were like, 'It's fine, there's just going to be 45 people' and I'm like, 'Yeah but the 45 people are going to be Harry Styles and Dua Lipa; that's so scary!'"

On the night, Olivia performed a haunting, but soaring, low-key version of 'drivers license' accompanied by harp and piano. It wowed all the celebrities – now fully fleshed Livies themselves – in the crowd, including Ed Sheeran who declared "I love Olivia Rodrigo!" shortly after. The performance helped install *Sour* at the top of the UK album chart.

The BRITs show was notable for more than being Olivia's first big gig, it was also the night she got to meet her idol, Taylor Swift,

"I DON'T WANT TO DIVULGE TOO MUCH BECAUSE IT'S PERSONAL, BUT TAYLOR TALKS A LOT ABOUT HOW YOU MAKE YOUR OWN LUCK IN THE WORLD, AND WHEN YOU DO KIND THINGS TO OTHERS, GOOD THINGS COME YOUR WAY. IT'S SO NICE TO BE WELCOMED INTO THE MUSIC INDUSTRY AND SO GREAT TO BE SUPPORTIVE OF OTHER WOMEN AND TAYLOR IS ABSOLUTELY THE KINDEST INDIVIDUAL IN THE WHOLE WORLD."

Olivia, on Taylor Swift's letter

ABOVE: President Joe Biden and Olivia pose with their Ray Ban Aviators in the White House's Oval Office, Washington, D.C., 14 July 2021.

BELOW LEFT: Olivia discusses the COVID-19 vaccine from the White House's Press Briefing Room, Washington, D.C., 14 July 2021.

BELOW: Vice President Kamala Harris praises Olivia's role as the voice of a generation, The White House, Washington D.C., 14 July 2021.

"IT'S WEIRD TO THINK ABOUT PEOPLE LIKE ED SHEERAN LOOKING AT MY SPOTIFY AND TURNING ON MY SONGS. THAT'S SO CRAZY!"

OPPOSITE: Olivia is 'good 4 u' at the 2021 MTV Video Music Awards, New York, 12 September 2021.

ABOVE: Olivia arrives at the 2021 BRIT Awards, London, 11 May 2021, where she met her idol, Taylor Swift!

for the first time. The pair were snapped together, and Olivia posted the photo on her Insta with a row of crying face emojis and a caption: "Brits were a dream! Never want to leave!!!"

Leave she did later that night, but she returned to London's O2 Arena in 2022, this time picking up her first ever BRIT award with her track 'good 4 u' winning International Song of the Year. Collecting her trophy, Olivia said, "Last year at the BRITs was my first performance ever so to get this award is so surreal."

Olivia's second ever live performance was equally as daunting – and haunting – as her first, proving once again just how swift Olivia's ascension to stardom has been. Beamed across small screens to an audience of millions, Olivia's sophomore show was on *Saturday Night Live,* the iconic U.S. comedy show. "I just had no idea how I would react to that kind of audience and that sort of pressure. I was like, 'Am I just going to go up there and freeze up?' Because it was literally my second performance. I had no idea. So it was kind of anxiety-inducing, but it was so much fun. I think live music is such an important part of life and obviously something that we've all been really missing in our lives."

She ended the Year of Olivia – 2021 – by celebrating the announcement of her *Sour* Tour – her first musical jaunt around the world. An eagerly awaited event that had been delayed due to the pandemic and Olivia's filming commitments for season 3 of *HSMTMTS.* The 48-show tour will kick-off in Portland in April 2022 and visit 33 major cities around the U.S and Canada before heading to Europe, with performances in Germany, France, Ireland and the UK. Naturally, all shows sold out in seconds. Some fans even reported being in queues of 90,000 people when they went on sale. That's Beatlemania levels of fan-mania!

The prospect of touring excited Olivia as much as her Livvies. "IT'S FINALLY HAPPENING" she tweeted when the news was official. "Been waiting so long to perform these songs live," she wrote on Insta. "This is my very first tour and I'm so nervous but so excited to sing and dance the night away with you all!!! If you weren't able to get tickets this time around there will be more tours in the future and I can't wait to see you then!!! Thank u to all my incredible fans."

After 18 months of seeing the world through a laptop, Olivia will be able to meet her Livvies live and loud and in person. But, rather than go big, Olivia has decided to mount a small-scale attack on cities, preferring to fill theatres, including the legendary Greek in L.A. and New York's Radio City Music Hall, rather than soulless

"'DRIVERS LICENSE' WAS THE FIRST SONG THAT I WROTE WHERE I WAS LIKE, 'OH WOW, THIS ACTUALLY REALLY CAPTURES HOW I FEEL TO A T.' AND IT WAS SUCH AN OVERWHELMING FEELING THAT WAS SO HARD TO EXTERNALIZE. AND I REMEMBER WRITING THAT SONG AND BEING LIKE, 'WOW, I FEEL REALLY GOOD ABOUT THAT.'

BOTH PICTURES: Olivia wins Song of the Year for 'drivers licence' at the 2021 MTV Video Music Awards, New York, 12 September 2021.

"I TRULY DON'T FEEL LIKE MY BRAIN CAN PROCESS ALL OF IT. I SEE ALL THE NUMBERS, BUT IT DOESN'T REALLY SINK IN TOTALLY, I'M SORT OF IN A STATE OF DISBELIEF."

arenas or stadiums. "I don't think I should skip any steps," Olivia said. She has chosen to get up close and intimate with her fans the first time out, rather than take the money and run. Another reminder that Olivia is unlike any other star seen in the sky lately. Unlike her peers, Ed Sheeran, or Phoebe Bridgers, or Billie Eilish, Olivia won't be alone on stage. She's taking her band with her. "It's all girls," Olivia announced. "I feel like I didn't get to see enough of that when I was a kid," she said.

With five years of ever-increasing fame behind her, Olivia has finally amassed a large, loyal and loving fanbase the world over. However, with great fame comes great responsibility. Today, the most important thing for Olivia is to be honest and real with her fans, because it is her authenticity, her realness, that elevated her, and a quality that makes her a vital role model in today's society which often feels as divided as it united. Olivia Rodrigo unites people, but in order to do so, she has to divide herself. Such is the cruel monster of fame. "Something that I learned very early on is the importance of separating person versus persona. When people who don't know me are criticizing me, they're criticizing my persona, not my person," Olivia said. "But that's really difficult, though, too, because my persona is being as genuine and honest as I possibly can, so it's this weird dichotomy."

In order to be the best role model she can be to her fans, Olivia's promise to herself is to flourish within fame, without losing herself

OPPOSITE: Attending the 2022 Brit Awards in London in a sparkly silver dress. Olivia won International Artist of the Year, and International Song of the Year.

ABOVE: Olivia picks up her first major international award at the BRIT Awards 2022, London, 8 February 2022.

to it. And that means ignoring the negative aspects of social media. Or, as Olivia puts it: "It helps to not look at that shit." In fact, Olivia went one step further and asked a friend to set up a child lock on her phone so that she can only log in to the apps for a maximum of 30 minutes a day. "Which is honestly the biggest blessing," Olivia said. "You're literally not meant to know what everyone is saying about you at all times."

Olivia's approach to social media is refreshing in an age that is seemingly besotted with maximizing its potential. "Putting out music in the age of social media can be really daunting, and I think people hold young women to an incredibly unrealistic standard. I don't think we as human beings are supposed to know what thousands of people think about what we wore or what we said or how we talk. I think having that separation is really important – realizing that that's not real life. That world that is created online, it's just one facet of this very big human existence." Beautifully said, Olivia!

The timing of the COVID-19 pandemic also helped Olivia keep her feet on the ground, allowing her to stay focused on what mattered, staying at home with her family, and not getting lost in the madness of sudden ridiculous fame – a thought that occupied Olivia's mind when it all started kicking off. "I was seeing all of these records being broken, all these people streaming the song and loving it, but at the same time, I wasn't actually able to meet anyone that was listening to it. I wasn't able to play a show or anything like that," said Olivia. "Experiencing the success of 'drivers license' in isolation was really great for my psyche and mental health. If I had been in L.A. with all these people while the song was getting big, then I would have put more pressure on myself to make the rest of the album as successful as that song," she said.

With support from her peers and her fans on her side, Olivia is now focusing on the next stage of her flourishing career. One thing she know for sure – it's been a wild ride already! "I'm just taking this day by day," she said. "It's all such a whirlwind at the moment, but it all comes down to the fact I just really love writing songs. I'm always writing, because it's the way I process my emotions. It never feels like work to me in that regard,"
she says. Let's hope it never stops, but for now Olivia knows her priorities – continuing to live her life as she wants – because what's true to her, will be true to her fans. And will keep her real.

"Now that *Sour* is out, I'm going to take a vacation somewhere on the beach with a lot of sun. I think that's super important, too. I was talking to somebody the other day, and they were like, 50 per cent of our jobs is writing songs and the other 50 per cent is living

a life to write songs about. You can't just spend all of your time in the studio or on tour, because what are you going to write your songs about? You sort of become out of touch with reality. So I'm definitely trying to keep that in mind as I go into my second album."
We can't wait.

At the beginning of 2022, Olivia moved out of her mom and dad's house in L.A. and now lives alone. She now has a room with her piano in that she can go to write songs and escape the world. "I love it," she said. "I also just don't know how to take care of myself, though. I don't know what to buy from the grocery store or how to clean up after myself, I realized. It's been a learning experience."

Olivia's journey into the future is unwritten, and where her next album takes her, and what it sounds like, or how successful it will be, nobody knows – yet. All that Olivia's fans know for certain is that they are on this amazing adventure with her. And

"I JUST TURNED 18, SO THERE ARE SO MANY NORMAL TEENAGE THINGS THAT I'M REALLY EXCITED TO DO. THERE'S SO MUCH IN LIFE THAT I HAVE TO LEARN AND SO MANY EXPERIENCES TO BE HAD. SO I'M HONESTLY MOST EXCITED FOR THAT. I LOVE GROWING UP. I FEEL LIKE I GET HAPPIER WITH AGE, SO HOPEFULLY THAT'S A TREND THAT CONTINUES."

OPPOSITE: Posing for selfies with fans during the 2021 American Music Awards, California, 21 November 2021.

ABOVE: Proud day: Olivia accepts the 2022 Woman of the Year award at *Billboard*'s prestigious Women in Music ceremony, California, 2 March 2022.

"I'M JUST GOING TO BECOME A BETTER SONGWRITER AND KNOW WHAT I WANT TO SAY MORE... I THINK THAT'S ACTUALLY A REALLY FUN, EXCITING PART OF BEING IN THE SPACE THAT I'M REALLY ENCOURAGED TO SORT OF HAVE DIFFERENT ERAS AND REINVENT YOURSELF."

they can't wait to see where her fairy-tale life takes her next. Olivia, of course, has a masterplan: "I just wanna be 30, in a cool mid-century modern house with two babies and a husband, writing songs that I like, and having brunch with my girls on the weekends."

Will her next dream come true too? Of course! And we can't wait to hear her songs about motherhood and girly brunches because without a doubt they'll be pop classics too – it's just the way she writes them.

OPPOSITE: The star arrives! Olivia at the premiere of *Driving Home 2 U* – her documentary following the making of *Sour*, California, 24 March 2022.

ABOVE: Avril Lavigne awards Olivia Songwriter of the Year at the Variety Hitmakers ceremony, California, 7 December 2021.

PICTURE CREDITS

The publishers would like to thank the following sources for their kind permission to reproduce the pictures in this book.

Alamy Stock Photo: Everett Collection Inc 11BR, 17R; Jennifer Graylock/INSTAR Images LLC 32; ZUMA Press, Inc. 48

Getty Images: Jenny Anderson 20, 25, 29BR; Paul Archuleta/FilmMagic 7; David M. Benett 46; Tommaso Boddi 14B, 60-61; Isaac Brekken 38, 40, 42-43; Gilbert Carrasquillo/GC Images 43R; Mike Coppola 4; Rick Diamond 10R; Rodin Eckenroth 14-15; Steven Ferdman 11T; FOX Image Collection 13T; Rich Fury 24, 62-63; Frazer Harrison 3TL, 27, 28-29; Mat Hayward 33; Dave J Hogan 34T; Samir Hussein/WireImage 56; JMEnternational 36BL, 36-37, 39, 41TR, 53, 57; Michael Kovac 61BR; Jeff Kravitz/FilmMagic 5; Kevin Mazur 45, 52, 54L, 62BR; Jamie McCarthy 10BR; Emma McIntyre 59; Rachel Murray 17T; Alberto E. Rodriguez 18TR; John Shearer 54-55; Chip Somodevilla 3R; Amy Sussman/Instagram and Facebook's Creator Week 41B; Denise Truscello 34B, 47; Mike Windle 12; Matt Winkelmeyer 49, 58; Kevin Winter 8-9

Shutterstock: 26; OfficialCharts.com 35; John Salangsang/BEI 30-31; Joe Seer 16; Dan Steinberg/Invision/AP 44; Michael Vi 11L; Susan Walsh/AP 51L; Walt Disney Pictures/Kobal 13B, 18B, 19B, 21, 22-23; White House/News Pictures 51T, 51B
Elements used throughout are all © Shutterstock

Every effort has been made to acknowledge correctly and contact the source and/or copyright holder of each picture. Any unintentional errors or omissions will be corrected in future editions of this book.

"THIS IS MY BIGGEST DREAM COME TRUE."